Thoughts with tea

Leslie Johnson

BookLeaf Publishing

Presentation by *BookLeaf Publishing*

Web: www.bookleafpub.com

E-mail: info@bookleafpub.com

ISBN: 9789357697248

First edition 2023

DEDICATION

To my life, my boys.

They do not know the strength they give me to get up each morning and strive to carry on and better myself.

Safe

To feel warm and secure
What does it mean
A roof over our head where we know we can
stay, no fear of having to no where to stay.
Food on the table to nourish our being and books
to read to feed the brain
A stable job to provide this and more without
fear of persecution within those four walls. They
say words don't hurt but the sadness inside, is
more than the physical sustained through the
day. Still finding my way on the ladder I climb,
so I fool others to think I know who I am. What
happens if I am sick and cannot work, who takes
care of the house and the food for the child.

To be alone has a strength of its own and takes a
while to really take hold, so long to grow and
really believe only to be weakened by strangers
who take what they want,
 be it in words or by actions they really care not
For some it's a game that brings in the rain.

The fear of a child who is out on their own, did I
teach them well and will they come home, I fear
the calls or knocks on the door, to wake me up
from my parental sleep, met with dreaded news

no one wants to hear I pray this moment will
never appear

To feel safe and secure is what we all want, but
to worry is love and that's worth way more. A
hug from a child takes the worry away and they
do not know how safe that love makes me feel.
One hug melts away the worries for a while and
gives me the strength to face another day.

Blood moon

Blood Moon

Blood Moon in the sky is the talk of the day
The glow of the shadows not a cloud in the sky.

For the sun and the earth and the moon to align
And to watch the light diminish is a wonderful
sight.

The stars that glow and twinkle above so many
more hidden are from sight, so far away that
light does not reach, how can we think that we
have such might.
Three year till we see such a site again, where
will I be or will I still care.
Right now I sit and ponder this view, the Blood
Moon

So much for one day

The days grow longer, and the night even
shorter, it's been a long year but that's nothing
new.
I remember the times when the years seemed so
long, but they are fading away like an old
Polaroid.
The days are routine it never seems to change, to
work, back home, to bed and repeat. Is this what
makes the year soles us by? We forget to stop
and breathe for a while.
As the days grow longer the time comes yet
closer, the planning, the cooking the shopping to
boot.
The weekends now booked with smiles and the
cheers, yet inside is filled with the looming
dread. The lawns have grown long and the paths
to be cleared, inside there is hunting of foods to
be found.
The decisions need making as it's crunch time
now, what colours, what food what gifts to be
bought.
The tree is found and all seems well, till finally
it's time to place the final star, who gets the
honour, the mighty star, you know an argument
is not too far.

The gifts are chosen and hiding well, and menu is sorted, well so we hope. The panic in stores as the scramble begins looking to check everything off the list. A well earnt rest is sorely needed but alas there is still more to come.

The house it tidied for the special guest, and children are shuffled off to their bed. The gifts now retrieved and the count must be even, and care must be taken to ensure all is comparable. The wrapping the tagging by now is an art and managed to be done with a stealthy ability.

For the sun starts to rise, it's finally time, the household is stirring then a flurry or running. That tidy home now covered in wrap and the cooking begins for the guests to arrive.

More wrap, more gifts, more food and more cheers, and more dishes but soon the sun will head down for its slumber.
The house once again is quiet and peaceful, time to sit and relax with my trusty old cuppa. How sleepy I am but happy in heart, to remember the joy and the laughter we shared.
As families we all do have peaks and troughs, but with our hats and our jokes all is now forgiven. Photos were taken and gifts were exchanged, St Nick would be proud of us all on this day.

Skateboard

The sound of the wheels,
Running on the pavement,
The gentle vibrations,
Sent up the legs.

Kick up the board,
Crossing the street,
The sounds of laughter,
Filling the air.

Children all skating,
Showing off tricks,
Life was so simple,
Riding the skateboard.

Balloons

A tall necked giraffe,
A long bodied dog,
A colourful flower,
A strong bubbled sabre.

Such little bits of plastic,
Filled simply with air,
Can bring so much joy,
To children all ages.

Tattoo

A stroke of the machine,
A soft gentle hum,
The sharp stabbing pain,
Embedding the ink,

Hours and hours,
Of sitting so still,
No movement allowed,
Tears roll on down.

All of the pain,
All of the cash,
Worth it in the end,
To see such a sight.

Such beautiful art,
To decorate flesh,
Individuality,
An amazing piece.

Emptiness

The bottles are empty,
The cups are all tipped,
Food on the floor,
Pictures askew.

The bottles are empty,
A void of blank space,
Resembling life,
And such harsh depression.

Bottles can be filled,
If you just stand them up,
Whatever is empty,
Can just be refilled.

The Empress

The queen of the crop,
A grandmothers love,
Cooks hundreds of meals,
Without hesitation.

She opens her arms,
For all of your friends,
She's there when you need her,
She helps you whenever.

The queen of the crop,
So strong and so fierce,
Don't come for her family,
She keeps a gun near.

Typewriters

History told,
History written,
Clicking and clacking,
A soft gentle ding.

The greatest of authors,
Have written their stories,
Cant make a mistake,
Or the page is all gone.

History told,
History written,
A typewriters dream,
For one last long story.

Mother Nature

To nourish, to feed, to hedge and to clipper, to
mow and to edge and wonder why bother.
My one day a week is filled to the brim yet the
garden demands all that's left of my time.
My bones do so ache as time takes it's toll,I miss
that one day as the clouds did ……..
Next week I say I'll get to it, but alas that next
time again it did rain.
I look with fear as the path disappears and begs
for attention which I do not hand out.
I feel the judges and unfair stares and shame
surrounds when someone walks by.
But wait what's that, a bee? And a beetle, next
thing a butterfly on flowers that grew when not
kept at bay.
My gardens alive with beautiful creatures and
those stares turned to wonder at what is now
there.
A home for the critters we don't always see as
we trim and cut and make it our way. Mother
Nature took over and created a sight and we all
see her grow and she'd always planned.
I leave her now and relax on my day and watch
and enjoy such a beautiful site. Now worry free
by bones get a rest, and I relax for a day and
leave her to the rest.

Best Friend

The keys in the door and I hear the excitement
inside,
It's been a long day so far and it's far from over,
dinner to be cooked and planning still to come,
I'm exhausted and drained but that greeting I
receive when I walk in the door makes it all
worthwhile.
With kisses and cuddles he is so glad I'm home
And becomes my shadow till it is time for bed.
His tail goes mad any time I am near, and he's
always ready for a cuddle on the sofa.
With the children grown up and feeling alone,
it's easy so see why a dog is a man's best friend.
He is a constant companion and will lend an ear
after a long hard day he will sit and listen, he
loves a play but also a snuggle and doesn't mind
the odd treat from my dinner.

Success

What is success I heard someone ask,
Is it money, a home or a child to hold?
Success for us all is always different, we live our
lives and try to aim high, to buy cars and trinkets
and be ahead of the game, a house so big that
you could get lost. To walk in a store and not
look at the price is that what it means to say you
succeed?
A holiday a year, a plane trip a yacht, golf
lessons and afternoons you can take off of work,
does this make you happy ? Do you still dream
for more?
But what of those who do not dream does that
mean that do not succeed?
For I see in them in inner glow, greatful for love
and simply lead lives, they do not reach power
or what some perceive as it, yet they have such a
glow inside when you see, for success to them is
a simple thing, being loved and to love, a roof
overhead and enough food to share. This in itself
is success beyond measure, an inner peace that
cannot be bought, they do not need trinkets or
money to burn they are happy in themselves and
do not need more. For this is success and what
people forget, to live and be happy which love in
your heart

My time

A cup, a mug, cream or lemon, kettle or pot, leaf or in a bag the chooses are endless decisions to make.
Earl Grey, Darjeeling, bush or roboost, peppermint or Jasmine, camomile or fruit flavoured.
In a pot or a plunger or good old kettle depends on the day and time left to savour.

For me it's an Earl Grey with milk and two sugar, the stress of the day now doesn't seem to matter. My mind slows right down and the day fades away, I sit outside and feel the breeze on my arms, the quiet of night with a tea in my hand, I know that tomorrow is a day I can face.

The change in the air

The change in the air as the season changes,
houses are decorated with festive cheer.
An evening walk is dull no longer, with
twinkling lights and view has changed.
The garlands are hung and the baubles are
placed, the fences and doorways now all do
twinkle.
With seasons greetings and holiday cheer, there
is no way not to fill up with hope.
The year may have been long but there is no
more to fear, the magic of St Nick has begun to
appear.
The magic of Christmas makes ill will fade
away, excitement it grows with each passing
day, for its friends and family and way too much
food. Each house is adorned and trees are all
placed, stress of the year replaced with
Christmas cheer.

Nature and nurture

Standing alone, a world all around, she seems so
tall, though not straight and conforming.
She can be guide or shelter, be a tower of
strength, a ladder, a home a sight to beholden.

A seed was once planted with the future in mind,
now firmly rooted it gives more each passing
year. Bend and change shape grow upwards and
out, branches get broken but soon do regrow.
Onwards and upwards each notch makes it
stronger, for children do climb and the birds she
gives shelter.
In winds she may bend and lose all her leaves,
no worry as she's planted her roots oh so deep.
In Spring she regrows a sight to behold, so green
with new leaves, and new branches appearing.
Its trunk may turn and twist and bend here and
there, but her strength and her hold can not be
mistaken. She will stand firm and all who do see
her, know they are safe with her as their shelter.

Fears

It's too scary, I can't do it
It's too high, I'm too scared.
I will do it if you do it,
Let's go together.
Climb over the side and take a deep breath
Step out and squeal
Splash we made it
It was so much fun
One more time, the fear has gone
Back up the rocks and onto the bridge, what
seemed so high now seems so fun,
So one more turns into more and more
flips and spins to swim back to the shore

The ceiling

Am I too broken? Are my wings clipped?
Can I break through, I ask everyday.

The ceiling is glass but can we push through,
It is there by default or all in our mind?

We are used to the glare and knives we dodge
All carefully aimed to keep us where we are.

A title is given but is it respected,
Told to smile and nurture along as we climb,
But when we are there we are told to change
tact, don't give power away but still keep your
smile

Too tired to go on, do we keep up the fight?
Hell yeah that we do, break away that glass
because we're here to stay!

The fence

The line that is drawn from the neighbour to me
The wooden pails that stand mighty tall
It's weathered and but still draws a curious eye.

For in the wood some faces appear,
An owl over here, or two eyes over there.
Have you ever just looked at a wooden fence,
The knots and the lines the natural decor.

For when you see and study the fence,
no longer a barrier but an interesting sight,
So next time your out take a curious mind
and count how many faces you can make in the
pails

The war

smoke filled the air
cries of people everywhere
people dying over here
children crying over there

lost toys on the floor
collapsed building all around
the planes roar beyond
tanks and soldiers fill the streets

toppled trees with dead leaves
wars rage for several years
whiles people's eyes fill with tears
this is warfare